First Aid and Medical Courses Criteria

Proficiency in Elementary First Aid

Proficiency in Medical First Aid

Proficiency in Medical Care

Medical Care Updating Training Requirements

First Edition published 2014
Revised 2015

ISBN 978-1-85609-702-4

© UK Chamber of Shipping/Merchant Navy Training Board, 2015

British Library Cataloguing in Publication Data

A catalogue record for this book is available from the British Library.

Printed and bound in Great Britain by Charlesworth Press, Wakefield

Published by Witherby Seamanship

A division of Witherby Publishing Group Ltd
4 Dunlop Square, Livingston,
Edinburgh, EH54 8SB,
Scotland, UK

Tel No: +44(0)1506 463 227

Email: info@emailws.com
Web: www.witherbys.com

CONTENTS

Section One	Introduction	1
Section Two	Proficiency in elementary first aid course criteria	5
Section Three	Proficiency in medical first aid course criteria	9
Section Four	Proficiency in medical care course criteria	13
Section Five	Medical care updating training course criteria	17
Annex A	MCA approval of short courses	19
Annex B	STCW Code:	
	(i) Table A-VI/1-3	20
	(ii) Table A-VI/4-1	21
	(iii) Table A-VI/4-2	22
Annex C	Instructor/assessor qualification and experience requirements	24
Annex D	Specimen certificates:	
	(i) Proficiency in elementary first aid	25
	(ii) Proficiency in medical first aid	26
	(iii) Proficiency in medical care	27
	(iv) Proficiency in medical care updating training	28

1. What this document is about

1.1 This document provides the criteria for the development of courses to deliver training in elementary first aid, medical first aid and medical care on board ship.

1.2 Training courses developed in line with these criteria, delivered at centres approved by the Maritime and Coastguard Agency (MCA), will cover:
- Elementary first aid (section 2);
- Medical first aid (section 3);
- Medical care (section 4);
- Medical care updating training (section 5) – an EU-specific requirement for service on EU registered vessels.

1.3 The specifications described in this document have been developed by the Merchant Navy Training Board (MNTB) in conjunction with the Maritime and Coastguard Agency (MCA).

1.4 The MCA has agreed with the MNTB that the specifications described in this document will satisfy the requirements for approved training. Conditions for MCA approval of short courses are contained in Annex A, which should be used in conjunction with the MCA guide to approval of regulatory training requirements.

1.5 The national occupational standards relating to this training are:

A16 – Provide medical services on board a vessel.

There is also a suite of Maritime Studies Qualifications which contain units relevant to this training; the specific units are:
- Emergency first aid in response to maritime accidents or medical emergencies;
- Provide medical first aid on board a vessel;
- Take charge of medical care on board a vessel.

2. Why these criteria have been developed

2.1 These criteria have been developed to deliver education and training covering first aid and medical care to meet specific parts of the regulatory requirements of Tables A-VI/1-3, A-VI/4-1 and A-VI/4-2 of the Annex to the International Convention on Standards of Training, Certification and Watchkeeping for Seafarers (STCW), 1978, hereafter referred to as STCW. It also covers the medical care updating training specific to the EU and as identified in EC Directive 92/29 EEC and part 6 of the MCA Training and Certification Guidance – MGN 96 (M).

3. Who the training is aimed at

3.1 This training is required by seafarers seeking certification under:
- a. STCW Regulation VI/I – basic training or instruction for seafarers employed or engaged in any capacity on board ship on the business of that ship as part of the ship's complement as appropriate;
- b. STCW Regulation VI/4 – training for seafarers who are designated to provide medical first aid on board ship;
- c. STCW Regulation VI/4 – training for seafarers who are designated to take charge of medical care on board ship;
- d. EU Council Directive 92/29 EEC as interpreted by the MCA – training required for masters and other persons in charge of medical care on UK or EU-flag vessels who are required to undertake refresher training every five years.

4. Aims of the training

4.1 The overall aim is to provide seafarers with the necessary knowledge, understanding and proficiency to carry out designated first aid and medical duties in accordance with international regulations.

4.2 Where training is provided to comply with EC92/29, additional training in the use of category C stores is required. In this instance the training centre should issue a separate/combined certificate to show the training has been completed.

5. Training plans

5.1 Centres will need to present their training plans as part of the approval process. Centres are encouraged to fully engage learners in the learning process using interactive teaching methods supported by appropriate use of one or more of the following:
- demonstration;
- team exercises.

5.2 The training plans must:
a. define education and training objectives and related standards of competence to be achieved;
b. identify the levels of knowledge, understanding and skills appropriate to the examinations and assessments required under these criteria.

6. Training day

6.1 A training day is defined as one which has no more than eight contact hours and cannot be in excess of 10 hours, including relevant breaks.

7. Assessment requirements

7.1 Assessment must be organised so that learners can, through demonstration and examination, show that they meet the competences stipulated, as identified in the tables in Annex B, and in accordance with the methods for demonstrating competence shown in column 3 of the tables and the criteria for evaluating competence in column 4.

7.2 The assessment system, methods and practice must be valid, reliable and authentic.

7.3 Each learner shall receive an assessment plan at the start of the training.

7.4 The assessment system should support appeals made by learners against assessment decisions.

7.5 A variety of sources of evidence may be used and must include evidence of learners' ability to meet the criteria for evaluating competence.

7.6 A range of direct observation, oral questioning, simulation and role play are considered ideal approaches to generating much of the evidence required.

7.7 Assessment must be formally documented and be made available for verification audits.

8. Qualifications of instructors and assessors

8.1 Instructors and assessors are required to be qualified in accordance with the requirements of Regulation I/6 STCW. Guidance on relevant qualifications and experience required to deliver and assess the training is given in Annex C.

9. Facilities and equipment

9.1 Training centres seeking approval will need to demonstrate availability of classrooms or equivalent facilities for general and theoretical instruction, suitably equipped with teaching and learning aids and designed to enable each learner to fully engage in the learning process.

9.2 All facilities must be maintained and where appropriate, inspected and tested in accordance with applicable regulations, current standards and manufacturers recommendations.

10. Certification

10.1 The training centre will issue a certificate to learners who have successfully demonstrated competence in all specified areas. The certificate will be in the relevant format provided in Annex D, of this document. A certificate cannot be issued prior to approval of the training by the MCA.

11. Health and Safety: conduct of training

11.1 All training centres must adhere to applicable regulations made under the Health and Safety at Work Act 1974, as amended, and take proper account of the advice given in associated guidance documents and 'Approved Codes of Practice'. Outside the UK, training centres must adhere to relevant national legislation.

11.2 Training centres are required to make assessments of any potential risks to the health and safety of staff and learners that may be associated with their activities. They are also required to identify, implement, monitor and review effective measures for minimising and controlling risks.

11.3 Centres are required to make effective arrangements for dealing with any emergency, incident or accident that may occur during the course of training. In the UK, the foregoing is required in accordance with the Management of Health and Safety at Work Regulations 1999, as amended.

11.4 The safety of learners and staff delivering training must be ensured at all times.

11.5 Practical exercises should be designed and delivered solely to meet the course criteria.

11.6 Centres must draw up their own safe working procedures to meet statutory Health and Safety obligations.

Aim

To give all persons intending to go to sea the education and training in elementary first aid to meet the Knowledge, Understanding and Proficiency (KUP) requirements set out in the following:

Table A-VI/1-3

Function: Elementary first aid
Competence: Take immediate action upon encountering an accident or other medical emergency

Entry requirements

Training centres must ensure, through pre-course information and screening, that learners are fit to participate in all aspects of the training. If there is any doubt as to an individual's ability to participate in such exercises an appropriate risk assessment should be carried out to determine what is required in order to proceed in a safe manner. Training centres may consider utilising the ENG1 medical certificate, or equivalent, as an indicator of fitness.

Outcomes

There are two outcomes to the training:

Outcome 1:   The learner understands what to do in case of an accident or medical emergency on board.
Outcome 2:   The learner is able to apply elementary first aid techniques.

Staff to learner ratio

The trainer to learner ratio should not exceed 1:12 for practical sessions. All training and instruction should be given, and assessments carried out, by personnel qualified to give instruction in first aid. This includes personnel that have current medical registration with the GMC or equivalent, NMC current registration to practice as an RGN or equivalent, a paramedic with current registration with the Health Professionals Council or equivalent, a qualified First Aid Instructor holding a Medical First Aid certificate of not more than two years old, or equivalents acceptable to the MCA.

The training centre, having due regard to health and safety and the objectives of the training, should determine other staffing requirements.

Training duration

The training shall be not less than six contact hours and may be delivered in a number of ways, including:
  i. As a single programme of training covering all basic training, designed and delivered in an integrated way meeting all the outcomes;
  ii. As a stand-alone module, where required.

Facilities and equipment

Centres seeking approval will need to show that they can provide or have access to:
  i. A classroom or equivalent for general instruction and the theoretical aspects of the course, to include suitable presentation facilities and audio-visual aids (eg DVDs, posters, diagrams);
  ii. Current editions of the following publications available for reference by those undergoing the training:
   • Ship Captain's Medical Guide;
   • International Maritime Dangerous Goods (IMDG) Code including within the supplement Medical First Aid Guide for Use in Accidents involving Dangerous Goods (MFAG);
   • Voluntary Services First Aid Manual;
   • Relevant Merchant Shipping Notices.

iii. The following equipment:
- Relevant medical equipment as listed in Annex 1 of MSN 1768 (M+F) or subsequent amendments, under the following headings:
  - resuscitation equipment
  - dressings;
- First aid kits (as per the above MSN);
- Stretcher equipment (as per the above MSN);
- A minimum of one resuscitation manikin per four learners.

Conduct of the training

The training should be structured around the outcomes although centres should devise their own training schedules and detailed lesson plans to ensure effective and logical delivery of the subject matter and achieve the objectives of the training.

Practical training in first aid techniques must be provided as part of the course and each learner should be instructed and assessed in resuscitation techniques. Together with oral questioning, this will also provide evidence that can be used for the purposes of assessing achievement of the outcomes of the training.

Certification and documentation

A certificate cannot be issued prior to approval by the MCA. On achievement of the desired standard of competence, a certificate will be issued by the centre in the format shown in Annex D (i).

Where the training is delivered as part of a basic training course, a combined certificate of completion of training may be issued based on the format at Annex D (ii). The titles of each section must be included on the certificate.

OUTCOMES

Outcome 1

The learner understands what to do in case of an accident or medical emergency on board a vessel.

Learning objectives

1. Identify types of accidents and emergencies on board that may require first aid to be administered and the types of casualties that may arise.

2. Describe methods of raising the alarm and how the manner and timing would relate to different degrees of accident or emergency.

3. Identify the immediate measures to be taken when accidents or medical emergencies occur.

4. Prioritise actions required when providing first aid.

5. Outline the importance of minimising risk of further harm to self and casualty.

Outcome 2

The learner is able to apply elementary first aid techniques.

Learning objectives

1. Describe body structure and functions relating to elementary first aid.

2. Identify emergency first aid equipment and demonstrate its use, including improvisation of bandages.

3. Demonstrate maintenance of airway, breathing and circulation in a casualty requiring resuscitation and an unconscious or choking casualty.

4. Describe cause and recognition of shock and demonstrate its management.

5. Describe types of bleeding and demonstrate their control and management.

6. Describe cause and recognition of burns, scalds and accidents caused by electric current and demonstrate their management.

7. Demonstrate correct positioning of a casualty according to the injury.

8. Identify casualty rescue and transportation techniques.

Aim

To give seafarers who are designated to provide medical first aid on board ship the essential education and training to meet the Knowledge, Understanding and Proficiency (KUP) requirements set out in the following:

Table A-VI/4-1

Function: Medical first aid
Competence: Apply immediate first aid in the event of accident or illness on board

Entry requirements

There are no pre-requisites in terms of prior training. Learners who hold a certificate in Elementary First Aid must undertake this training in full in order to update and extend their knowledge and skills in current medical first aid procedures.

Training centres must ensure, through pre-course information and screening, that learners are fit to participate in all aspects of the training. If there is any doubt as to an individual's ability to participate in such exercises an appropriate risk assessment should be carried out to determine what is required in order to proceed in a safe manner. Training centres may consider utilising the ENG1 medical certificate, or equivalent, as an indicator of fitness.

Outcomes

There is one outcome to the training:

Outcome 1: The learner is able to apply immediate first aid to an injured casualty and a person suffering illness on board.

Staff to learner ratio

The trainer to learner ratio should not exceed 1:12 for practical sessions. All training and instruction should be given, and assessments carried out, by suitably qualified personnel e.g. registered nurse, registered medical practitioner, emergency medical technician, offshore/ambulance paramedic. This includes personnel that have current medical registration with the GMC or equivalent, NMC current registration to practice as an RGN, or equivalents acceptable to the MCA.

The training centre, having due regard to health and safety and the objectives of the training, should determine other staffing requirements.

Training duration

The training shall be not less than 28 contact hours over four days with at least 50% of the course devoted to practical exercises, using simulated casualties where necessary and appropriate.

Facilities and equipment

Centres seeking approval will need to show that they can provide or have access to:
   i. A classroom or equivalent for general instruction and the theoretical aspects of the course, to include suitable presentation facilities and audio-visual aids (eg DVDs, posters, diagrams);
   ii. Current editions of the following publications available for reference by those undergoing the training:
   - Ship Captain's Medical Guide;
   - International Maritime Dangerous Goods (IMDG) Code including within the supplement Medical First Aid Guide for Use in Accidents involving Dangerous Goods (MFAG);
   - Voluntary Services First Aid Manual;
   - Relevant Merchant Shipping Notices.

iii. The following equipment:

- Relevant medical equipment as listed in the Annex 1 of MSN 1768 (M+F) or subsequent amendments, under the following headings:
  - resuscitation equipment
  - dressings;
- First aid kits (as per the above MSN);
- Stretcher equipment (as per the above MSN);
- A minimum of one resuscitation manikin per four learners.

Conduct of the training

The training should be structured around the outcomes although centres should devise their own training schedules and detailed lesson plans to ensure effective and logical delivery of the subject matter and achieve the objectives of the training.

Practical training in first aid techniques must be provided as part of the course and each learner should be instructed and assessed in resuscitation techniques. Together with oral questioning, this will also provide evidence that can be used for the purposes of assessing achievement of the outcomes of the training.

Certification and documentation

A certificate cannot be issued prior to approval by the MCA. On achievement of the desired standard of competence, a certificate will be issued by the centre in the format shown in Annex D (iii).

Outcomes

Outcome 1

The learner is able to apply immediate first aid to an injured casualty and a person suffering illness on board.

Learning objectives

1. Describe body structure and functions relating to immediate first aid.

2. List the contents of the first aid kit and demonstrate use of the equipment.

3. Describe use of the Medical First Aid Guide, including treatment required as a result of accidents involving dangerous goods.

4. Identify the immediate measures to be taken when accidents, medical emergencies or illnesses occur, including prioritising actions to be taken and minimising risk of harm to self and casualty.

5. Describe how to manage illness on board.

6. Describe the procedures for maintaining hygiene when undertaking first aid, and demonstrate correct hand washing techniques.

7. Demonstrate maintenance of airway, breathing and circulation in a casualty requiring resuscitation, and an unconscious or choking casualty – including carrying out cardio-pulmonary resuscitation.

8. Demonstrate how to give appropriate first aid in accordance with recognised principles for illnesses related to chest pain, breathing problems, hypoglycaemia and poisoning.

9. Explain the procedures for getting radio medical advice and identify the information that needs to be provided to enable the most appropriate advice to be given.

10. Describe cause and recognition of shock and demonstrate its management.

11. Describe external and internal types of bleeding and demonstrate their control and management.

12. Describe how to identify the causes and severity of common types of burns and demonstrate their immediate management.

13. Describe the effect of extremes of heat and cold and demonstrate the management of related conditions, including heat exhaustion, heat stroke and hypothermia.

14. Describe types of spinal and musculo-skeletal injuries and demonstrate their immediate management.

15. Describe types of injury related to the head, chest and abdomen and demonstrate their management.

16. Demonstrate methods of caring for and monitoring ill persons.

17. Identify casualty rescue requirements and demonstrate appropriate transportation techniques.

Aim

To give seafarers who are designated to provide medical care on board ship the essential education and training to meet the Knowledge, Understanding and Proficiency (KUP) requirements set out in the following:

Table A-VI/4-2

Function: Medical care
Competence: Provide medical care to the sick and injured while they remain on board Participate in co-ordinated schemes for medical assistance to ships

Entry requirements

Those undertaking this training must have completed and been issued with a certificate covering Medical First Aid on Board Ship (Section A-VI/4-1 of STCW).

Training centres must ensure, through pre-course information and screening, that learners are fit to participate in all aspects of the training. If there is any doubt as to an individual's ability to participate in such exercises an appropriate risk assessment should be carried out to determine what is required in order to proceed in a safe manner. Training centres may consider utilising the ENG1 medical certificate, or equivalent, as an indicator of fitness.

Outcomes

There are 3 outcomes to the training:

Outcome 1:   The learner understands how to participate in the co-ordinated provision of medical care to a person on board.
Outcome 2:   The learner is able to assess and provide care to an ill person on board.
Outcome 3:   The learner is able to assess and provide care to an injured casualty on board.

Staff to learner ratio

The trainer to learner ratio should not exceed 1:12 for practical sessions. All training and instruction should be given, and assessments carried out, by suitably qualified personnel e.g. registered nurse, registered medical practitioner, emergency medical technician, offshore/ambulance paramedic. This includes personnel that have current medical registration with the GMC or equivalent, NMC current registration to practice as an RGN, Royal Navy Warrant Officer Medics or equivalents acceptable to the MCA.

The training centre, having due regard to health and safety and the objectives of the training, should determine other staffing requirements.

Training duration

The training shall be not less than 35 contact hours over 4½ days and at least 35% of the course should be devoted to practical exercises. It should be noted that the first aid aspects of the course will be by way of revision of previous learning, including that undertaken during the medical first aid course.

Facilities and equipment

Centres seeking approval will need to show that they can provide or have access to:

i.   A classroom or equivalent for general instruction and the theoretical aspects of the course, to include suitable presentation facilities and audio-visual aids (eg DVDs, posters, diagrams);
ii. Current editions of the following publications available for reference by those undergoing the training:
   - Ship Captain's Medical Guide;
   - International Maritime Dangerous Goods (IMDG) Code including within the supplement Medical First Aid Guide for Use in Accidents involving Dangerous Goods (MFAG);
   - Voluntary Services First Aid Manual;
   - Relevant Merchant Shipping Notices.

iii. The following equipment:
  - Medical equipment listed in Annex 1 of MSN 1768 (M+F) or subsequent amendments under the following headings:
    - resuscitation techniques
    - dressing and suturing equipment
    - instruments
    - immobilisation and setting equipment;
  - First aid kits (as per the above MSN);
  - Stretcher equipment (as per the above MSN);
  - A minimum of one resuscitation manikin per four learners;
  - Suitable models or surrogates for people to demonstrate suturing, passing a catheter, giving an intramuscular injection;
  - Telephone/intercom to stimulate information relay to bridge and for obtaining radio medical advice;
  - Demonstration ship medicine chest with appropriate medical log books and medication use records.

Conduct of the training

The training should be structured around the outcomes although centres should devise their own training schedules and detailed lesson plans to ensure effective and logical delivery of the subject matter and achieve the objectives of the training.

Practical training in medical care techniques and how to deal with illness and accidents must be provided as part of the course. Together with oral questioning, this will also provide evidence that can be used for the purposes of assessing achievement of the outcomes of the training.

Certification and documentation

A certificate cannot be issued prior to approval by the MCA. On achievement of the desired standard of competence, a certificate will be issued by the centre in the format shown in Annex D (iv).

Outcomes

Outcome 1

The learner understands how to participate in the co-ordinated provision of medical care to a person on board.

Learning objectives

1. Explain what the radio medical advice service is and how it operates.

2. Explain the procedures for obtaining radio medical advice and for participating in co-ordinated schemes for medical assistance to ships.

3. Identify the information that needs to be given to radio medical advice personnel about the ill or injured person that will enable them to provide the most appropriate advice, including vital signs and changes to them and monitoring data assembled for review by the RMS service doctor.

4. Demonstrate the procedures for transporting ill and injured persons from the ship to a place of safety, including urgent evacuation, and describe how to manage a death at sea.

5. Describe the procedures for co-operating with port health authorities or with port health care providers to arrange medical care for sick seafarers.

6. Describe communication methods and the requirements related to medical and medication records and international and national maritime medical regulations.

7. Describe how to provide protection against infection and the spread of diseases.

8. Identify the briefing requirements for newly embarked seafarers on first aid and medical arrangements on board.

9. Describe how to set up arrangements for, and identify the alarm criteria concerning, seriously ill or injured persons on board who need continuous care or observation.

Outcome 2

The learner is able to assess and provide care to an ill person on board.

Learning objectives

1. Describe the assessment and care of a person suffering illness at sea, including: methods of monitoring their condition and how to monitor and chart vital signs, covering pulse, temperature, blood pressure, breathing rate, state of consciousness.

2. Describe methods of providing pain relief.

3. Demonstrate how to give an intramuscular and a subcutaneous injection.

4. Demonstrate how to deal with medical conditions and their emergencies, including:
   - Conditions of the cardio vascular and respiratory systems;
   - Conditions relating to the abdomen; gynaecological, urinary and gastro intestinal systems, including passing an urinary catheter;
   - Conditions involving the head and neck; ear, nose and throat; dental and ophthalmic conditions;
   - Communicable diseases and sexually transmitted infections;
   - Illness related to substance misuse.

5. Describe how to recognise and deal with infections, including methods of prevention, monitoring and control.

6. Describe the use of medicines on board, including methods of storage, administration and record keeping.

7. Demonstrate the use of medical reference materials available on board to assist with assessment and care.

8. Describe the process of identifying new developments in diagnosis and treatment.

Outcome 3

The learner is able to assess and provide care to an injured casualty on board.

Learning objectives

1. Administer first aid and perform resuscitation techniques in accordance with current first aid procedures and practice.

2. Describe how to care for a rescued casualty until they recover or can be evacuated to shore.

3. Demonstrate the secondary management of wounds, covering methods of wound closure and bleeding control, including suturing a wound.

Introduction

This training is an EU-specific requirement to provide updating training every five years as identified by the EC Directive 92/29 EEC and part 6 of the MCA Training and Certification Guidance – MGN 96 (M) or subsequent amendments.

Where updating training is required, the individual can choose to undertake either this updating training course or the full Medical Care on Board Ship course, whichever best meets their needs.

Aim

To give masters and other persons designated to take charge of medical care on UK or EU-flag vessels who are required to undertake updating training in Proficiency in Medical Care on Board Ship every five years, the training set out in Table A-VI/4-2.

Entry requirements

Before commencing training, learners must either have received approved or recognised training in Proficiency in Medical Care on Board Ship (in accordance with Section A-VI/4-2 of the STCW Code) or hold a certificate of Updated Proficiency in Medical Care on Board Ship.

Outcomes

There is one outcome to the training:

Outcome 1: The learner is able to maintain the required standard of competence in providing medical care and first aid on board a vessel.

Staff to learner ratio

As per the medical care on board ship course requirements.

Training duration

The training shall be not less than 21 contact hours over 3 days and at least 50% of the course should be devoted to practical exercises.

Facilities and equipment

As required, taking account of the Medical Care on Board Ship course requirements.

Conduct of the training

As required, taking account of the Medical Care on Board Ship course requirements. Trainers must be aware of the latest developments in diagnosis and treatment.

Certification and documentation

A certificate cannot be issued prior to approval by the MCA. On achievement of the desired standard of competence, a certificate will be issued by the centre in the format shown in Annex D (v).

Outcome 1

The learner is able to maintain the required standard of competence in providing medical care on board a vessel.

Learning objectives

1. Describe how to use the equipment and medicines available on board.

2. Identify the sources of information and up to date techniques for providing medical care on board.

3. Explain the procedures for participation in co-ordinated schemes for medical assistance to ships, including Medical Advice by Radio.

4. Describe how to recognise and deal with infections, including methods of prevention, monitoring and control.

5. Demonstrate the assessment and care of a person suffering illness or injury, including on-going care and supervision until expert attention is available.

6. Demonstrate life-saving procedures for common life threatening situations.

7. Demonstrate methods of recognising, diagnosing and treating seriously ill persons, including common medical conditions and their emergencies and conditions associated with the respiratory, cardiac and abdominal systems.

8. Demonstrate methods of monitoring the condition of an ill person, including how to monitor and chart vital signs covering pulse, blood pressure, temperature, breathing rate, state of consciousness.

9. Describe methods of providing pain relief.

10. Demonstrate how to give an intramuscular and a subcutaneous injection.

11. Demonstrate how to deal with medical conditions and their emergencies, including:
    - Conditions of the cardio vascular and respiratory systems;
    - Conditions relating to the abdomen; gynaecological, urinary and gastro intestinal systems, including passing an urinary catheter;
    - Conditions involving the head and neck; ear, nose and throat; dental and ophthalmic conditions;
    - Communicable diseases and sexually transmitted infections;
    - Illness related to substance misuse.

12. Describe the procedures for arranging the evacuation of a patient.

13. Describe the record keeping requirements related to medical records and international and national maritime medical regulations.

14. Identify the latest new developments in diagnosis and treatment.

15. Describe how to keep up to date with changes and developments in diagnosis and treatment.

Annex A – Conditions for MCA Approval of Short Courses

1. Training centres offering training and assessment leading to the issue of a certificate of proficiency must be approved by the Maritime and Coastguard Agency.

2. MCA approval requirements are for a functional Quality Management System to be in place that ensures:
   a. Continued satisfactory delivery of the programme to the current standards, reflecting changes of technology and best practice;
   b. The training programme entry standards are met;
   c. The agreed assessment process is maintained;
   d. Only those who complete the training programme and meet any other necessary requirements are issued with certificates/documentary evidence;
   e. Certificates are issued in a format that meets the MCA requirements, as per the examples provided for the operational and management levels within sections two and three of this document;
   f. Records of certificates issued are securely maintained until the 70th birthday of the certificate holder or five years from the date of issue whichever is the longer;
   g. The record system enables authenticity of certificates to be verified and replacement certificates issued;
   h. Where approved for peripatetic delivery, formal assessment is carried out to ascertain the suitability of each venue and records of such assessment are retained for five years;
   i. The approving MCA Office is informed of dates, timing and venues of all courses delivered;
   j. Any changes made to the course content, facilities, equipment, training staff or other matter that may affect the delivery of the programme are reported to the approving Marine Office without delay.

3. Monitoring of the training programme by the MCA proves to be satisfactory.

4. Re-approval by the MCA is carried out within 5 years of the approval or re-approval. Such approval and re-approval will incur costs in line with the fees in force at that time.

5. Should the training establishment cease to trade then all records of certificates issued should be sent to the MCA to enable them to carry out the verification and replacement functions.

Relevant extracts of the STCW Code
Table A-VI/1-3
Specification of minimum standard of competence in elementary first aid

COLUMN 1	COLUMN 2	COLUMN 3	COLUMN 4
COMPETENCE	KNOWLEDGE, UNDERSTANDING AND PROFICIENCY	METHODS FOR DEMONSTRATING COMPETENCE	CRITERIA FOR EVALUATING COMPETENCE
Take immediate action upon encountering an accident or other medical emergency	Assessment of needs of casualties and threats to own safety Appreciation of body structure and functions Understanding of immediate measures to be taken in cases of emergency, including the ability to: .1 position casualty .2 apply resuscitation techniques .3 control bleeding .4 apply appropriate measures of basic shock management .5 apply appropriate measures in event of burns and scalds, including accidents caused by electric current .6 rescue and transport a casualty .7 improvise bandages and use materials in the emergency kit	Assessment of evidence obtained from approved instruction or during attendance at an approved course	The manner and timing of raising the alarm is appropriate to the circumstances of the accident or medical emergency The identification of probable cause, nature and extent of injuries is prompt and complete, and the priority and sequence of actions is proportional to any potential threat to life Risk of further harm to self and casualty is minimised at all times

Table A-VI/4-1
Specification of minimum standard of competence in medical first aid

COLUMN 1	COLUMN 2	COLUMN 3	COLUMN 4
COMPETENCE	KNOWLEDGE, UNDERSTANDING AND PROFICIENCY	METHODS FOR DEMONSTRATING COMPETENCE	CRITERIA FOR EVALUATING COMPETENCE
Apply immediate first aid in the event of accident or illness on board	First-aid kit Body structure and function Toxicological hazards on board, including use of the Medical First Aid Guide for Use in Accidents Involving Dangerous Goods (MFAG) or its national equivalent Examination of casualty or patient Spinal injuries Burns, scalds and effects of heat and cold Fractures, dislocations and muscular injuries Medical care of rescued persons Radio medical advice Pharmacology Sterilization Cardiac arrest, drowning and asphyxia	Assessment of evidence obtained from practical instruction	The identification of probable cause, nature and extent of injuries is prompt, complete and conforms to current first-aid practice Risk of harm to self and to others is minimized at all times Treatment of injuries and the patient's condition is appropriate and conforms to recognised first-aid practice and international guidelines

Table A-VI/4-2
Specification of minimum standard of competence in medical care

COLUMN 1	COLUMN 2	COLUMN 3	COLUMN 4
COMPETENCE	KNOWLEDGE, UNDERSTANDING AND PROFICIENCY	METHODS FOR DEMONSTRATING COMPETENCE	CRITERIA FOR EVALUATING COMPETENCE
Provide medical care to the sick and injured while they remain on board	Care of the casualty involving: .1 head and spinal injuries .2 injuries of ear, nose, throat and eyes .3 external and internal bleeding .4 burns, scalds and frostbite .5 fractures, dislocations and muscular injuries .6 wounds, wound healing and infection .7 pain relief .8 techniques of sewing and clamping .9 management of acute abdominal conditions .10 minor surgical treatment .11 dressing and bandaging Aspects of nursing: .1 general principles .2 nursing care Diseases, including: .1 medical conditions and emergencies .2 sexually transmitted diseases .3 tropical and infectious diseases Alcohol and drug abuse Dental care Gynaecology, pregnancy and childbirth Medical care of rescued persons Death at sea Hygiene	Assessment of evidence obtained from practical instruction and demonstration Where practicable, approved practical experience at a hospital or similar establishment	Identification of symptoms is based on the concepts of clinical examination and medical history Protection against infection and spread of diseases is complete and effective Personal attitude is calm, confident and reassuring Treatment of injury or condition is appropriate and conforms to accepted medical practice and relevant national and international medical guides The dosage and application of drugs and medication complies with manufacturers' recommendations and accepted medical practice The significance of changes in patient's condition is promptly recognised

COLUMN 1	COLUMN 2	COLUMN 3	COLUMN 4
COMPETENCE	KNOWLEDGE, UNDERSTANDING AND PROFICIENCY	METHODS FOR DEMONSTRATING COMPETENCE	CRITERIA FOR EVALUATING COMPETENCE
	Disease prevention, including: .1 disinfection, disinfestations, de-ratting .2 vaccinations Keeping records and copies of applicable regulations: .1 keeping medical records .2 international and national maritime medical regulations		
Participate in co-ordinated schemes for medical assistance to ships	External assistance, including: .1 radio medical advice .2 transportation of the ill and injured, including helicopter evacuation .3 medical care of sick seafarers involving co-operation with port health authorities or out-patient wards in port		Clinical examination procedures are complete and comply with instructions received The method and preparation for evacuation is in accordance with recognised procedures and is designed to maximise the welfare of the patient Procedures for seeking radio medical advice conform to established practice and recommendations

Annex C – Instructor/Assessor Qualification and Experience Requirements

All training and instruction should be given, and assessments carried out, by suitably qualified and experienced personnel. This annex provides guidance regarding the suitability and acceptability of qualifications and experience for personnel designated to carry out training, instruction or assessment in first aid and medical care courses. The list is not exhaustive, and suitable equivalent qualifications and experience will be considered.

Contextual awareness

All trainers and assessors should:
  i. Understand the specific objectives of the training;
  ii. Be familiar with the use and operation of the medical stores statutorily required to be carried on board ship;
  iii. Have an awareness of the operational environment on board and the national and international arrangements and procedures for medical care on board whilst ships are at sea, including radio medical advice;
  iv. Be able to demonstrate the currency of any professional registration or first aid qualification;
  v. Be able to demonstrate first aid and medical knowledge relevant to this training through a log book or portfolio of relevant professional development activity.

Instructional qualifications and experience

1. All trainers and assessors must hold a first aid qualification or professional medical registration.

2. All trainers and assessors should have:
   a. A knowledge of instructional techniques, training methods and training practice at least to the level of IMO Training for Instructors;
   b. An understanding of assessment methods and practice;
   c. Practical instructional and assessment experience.

Requirements for Training Centres

Training centres should have procedures in place to enable staff to update their knowledge of first aid and medical care, plus their knowledge of instruction and assessment techniques, in accordance with current CPD practice.

SPECIMEN CERTIFICATES
PROFICIENCY IN ELEMENTARY FIRST AID
(to be produced and registered locally by the Issuing Authority)

Certificate No: *[Unique identifier number allocated by Approved Training Centre]*

MCA Approval Certificate Number: *[issued by the MCA]*

Address and contact details including telephone and email of Issuing Authority *[Approved Training Centre]*

Certificate of Proficiency in
Elementary First Aid

This is to certify that *[full name of learner]*

Date of birth *[DD/MM/YYYY]*

Discharge Book Number or other National ID *[identify the document]*

has successfully completed a programme of training approved by the Maritime and Coastguard Agency as meeting the requirements laid down in:

Regulation VI/1, paragraph 1 and Section A-VI/1, paragraphs 2.1.3 of the STCW Convention and Code 1978, as amended

and has also met the additional criteria specified in the STCW Convention and Code, applicable to the issue of this certificate.

This Certificate is issued under the authority of the Maritime and Coastguard Agency of the United Kingdom of Great Britain and Northern Ireland, an executive agency of the Department for Transport.

Signature of Principal or Authorised Representative of the
Approved Training Centre

Issuing authority
stamp and date

Signature of person to whom this certificate was issued

Inquiries concerning this certificate should be addressed to the Issuing Authority at the address above.

SPECIMEN CERTIFICATE
PROFICIENCY IN MEDICAL FIRST AID
(to be produced and registered locally by the Issuing Authority)

Certificate No: *[Unique identifier number allocated by Approved Training Centre]*

MCA Approval Certificate Number: *[issued by the MCA]*

Address and contact details including telephone and email of Issuing Authority *[Approved Training Centre]*

Certificate of Proficiency in
Medical First Aid

This is to certify that *[full name of learner]*

Date of birth *[DD/MM/YYYY]*

Discharge Book Number or other National ID *[identify the document]*

has successfully completed a programme of training approved by the Maritime and Coastguard Agency as meeting the requirements laid down in:

Regulation VI/4, paragraph 1 and Section A-VI/4, paragraphs 1 to 3 of the STCW Convention and Code 1978, as amended

and has also met the additional criteria specified in the STCW Convention and Code, applicable to the issue of this certificate.

This Certificate is issued under the authority of the Maritime and Coastguard Agency of the United Kingdom of Great Britain and Northern Ireland, an executive agency of the Department for Transport.

Signature of Principal or Authorised Representative of the
Approved Training Centre

Issuing authority
stamp and date

Signature of person to whom this certificate was issued

Inquiries concerning this certificate should be addressed to the Issuing Authority at the address above.

SPECIMEN CERTIFICATE
PROFICIENCY IN MEDICAL CARE
(to be produced and registered locally by the Issuing Authority)

Certificate No: *[Unique identifier number allocated by Approved Training Centre]*

MCA Approval Certificate Number: *[issued by the MCA]*

Address and contact details including telephone and email of Issuing Authority *[Approved Training Centre]*

Certificate of Proficiency in Medical Care

This is to certify that *[full name of learner]*

Date of birth *[DD/MM/YYYY]*

Discharge Book Number or other National ID *[identify the document]*

has successfully completed a programme of training approved by the Maritime and Coastguard Agency as meeting the requirements laid down in:

Regulation VI/4, paragraph 2 and Section A-VI/4, paragraphs 4 to 6 of the STCW Convention and Code 1978, as amended

and has also met the additional criteria specified in the STCW Convention and Code, applicable to the issue of this certificate.

This Certificate is issued under the authority of the Maritime and Coastguard Agency of the United Kingdom of Great Britain and Northern Ireland, an executive agency of the Department for Transport.

Signature of Principal or Authorised Representative of the
Approved Training Centre

Issuing authority
stamp and date

Signature of person to whom this certificate was issued

Inquiries concerning this certificate should be addressed to the Issuing Authority at the address above.

SPECIMEN CERTIFICATE
UPDATED PROFICIENCY IN MEDICAL CARE
(to be produced and registered locally by the Issuing Authority)

Certificate No: *[Unique identifier number allocated by Approved Training Centre]*

MCA Approval Certificate Number: *[issued by the MCA]*

Address and contact details including telephone and email of Issuing Authority *[Approved Training Centre]*

**Certificate of Updated Proficiency
in Medical Care**

This is to certify that *[full name of learner]*

Date of birth *[DD/MM/YYYY]*

Discharge Book Number or other National ID *[identify the document]*

has successfully completed a programme of training approved by the Maritime and Coastguard Agency as meeting the requirements laid down in:

Table A-VI/4-2 of the STCW Convention and Code 1978, as amended

and has also met the requirements of article 5, paragraph 3 of EC Directive 92/29/EEC on the minimum safety and health requirements for improved medical treatment on board vessels.

This Certificate is issued under the authority of the Maritime and Coastguard Agency of the United Kingdom of Great Britain and Northern Ireland, an executive agency of the Department for Transport.

Signature of Principal or Authorised Representative of the
Approved Training Centre

Issuing authority
stamp and date

Signature of person to whom this certificate was issued

Inquiries concerning this certificate should be addressed to the Issuing Authority at the address above.